LITERARY ENGLAND

Photographs by David E. Scherman and

Descriptive Text by Richard Wilcox

LITERARY ENGLAND

PHOTOGRAPHS OF PLACES
MADE MEMORABLE
IN ENGLISH LITERATURE

By David E. Scherman & Richard Wilcox

A Preface by Christopher Morley

Published by RANDOM HOUSE New York

A Preface:
THE SENSE OF PLACE
by Christopher Morley

✳✳✳✳✳✳✳✳✳✳✳✳✳✳✳✳✳✳✳✳✳✳✳✳✳✳✳✳✳✳✳✳✳✳✳✳✳✳✳

ENGLAND is a land that made friends with herself; with her natural genius. Her political puberty began early. Prodigious biological shuffling, a climate that encouraged indoor meditation, and a landscape bewitched with bashful beauty—variously beautiful, but never spectacular—begot quicksilver fancy upon a carnal and sombre people. In that island of disillusioned and temperate humor, man has most continuously and eloquently recorded the mortal effort to rise above our own carcass—and still enjoy the carcass. "There'll always be an England" was one of the casual gnomes of this era, and that same England will always be to other nations a special paradox: at once a museum piece of ancient magic and the most diligently foresighted of modern democracies. Both Dr. Goebbels and the Chicago *Tribune* have frequently intoned a Litany for Britain; the only response has been grim cockney laughter.

There was a sign I used to see years ago on many pubs along the eastern docksides of London River. It said COURAGE'S STOUT. It was tragically prophetic; but also symbol and summary.

✳   ✳   ✳

The best substitute for eternity is perfect suggestion of the momentary. The mind is freakish in choosing the moment it would perpetuate. In a London paper (in 1930) among advertisements of Landed Estates I saw that the Earl of Verulam was offering for sale his great property at St. Albans, "including the historic ruins of Bacon's house...completely walled kitchen gardens . . . valuable watercress beds." Then to me that estate became real: lo, here the actual gardens where the first Verulam plotted his alleys of thyme and mint and cress. Now I see him forever pacing an appetizer on his sunset path, scheming simultaneously in English and Latin while he bruises the mint beds with his heel—"to have the pleasure when you walk or tread." Since first reading that scented passage even my Lord's meanest stratagem acquires a peppermint flavor.

Or I see Hazlitt—but we better let him see for himself. No one of our tongue has had keener sense of Place:

> . . . one day after a sultry walk in summer between Farnham and Alton. I was fairly tired out; I walked into an inn-yard (I think at the latter place). The room I entered opened into an old-fashioned garden, embellished with beds of larkspur and a leaden Mercury; it was wainscoted, and there was a grave-looking, dark-coloured portrait of Charles II hanging over the tiled chimney-piece. I had Love for Love in my pocket, and began to read; coffee was brought in a silver coffee-pot; the cream, the bread and butter, everything was excellent, and the flavour of Congreve's style prevailed over all.

These are mental pictures only, revived in selfish enjoyment. How much more mystery, and a deep riddling pleasure, in the photographer's image of any scene, whether familiar or strange. We con it over, examine the accidents of light and pose. We enjoy for an instant that exquisite fix, Fitz-Omar's "moment's halt, the momentary taste of being." We are granted, in the eye and the anxious mind, what we so fondly suppose we desire: permanence. Then to that wish for seeing steadily and whole is joined the pleasure of great words in alliance. It is a moment of pure feeling and complicated joy. We are in a mood to relish such wise dreamers as George Santayana:

> The human mind at best is a sort of song; the music of it runs away with the words, and even the words, which pass for the names of things, are but poor wild symbols for their unfathomed objects.*

The best prologue to this album of symbols would be in verse. It would be, if honest, reminiscent verse; when I was a boy on a bicycle exploring England,

* In the prologue of his *Soliloquies in England* (1922), a book of the rarest sensibility and surprise. He also treads on mint.

more than thirty years ago, I wrote among earnest notes of ambition a memo that a wonderful textbook of English literature could be made with bicycle and kodak. I was always a great map-reader, and one of the astonishments of England to an American boy was how you could study one of Bartholomew's glorious survey-sheets at random and always come upon some place-name that started induced resonance. It usually happened after you had left the neighborhood of what you might have wished to see. But still to spy over the green and pink and brown of Bartholomew's elevations, enlarging detail with a reading lens, brings landscape alive. It is like being in a plane—like being a skylark—hills, hedgerows and villages are spread in depth beneath you, and a name that was only an allusion is suddenly a Place. The Shakespeare Cliff or the stripling Thames, Sherwood Forest or Malvern Hills, Runnymede or Merrow Down, these are not just "literature," they are human lives and thoughts. To me the best Basic English is always the map.

So I think with gratitude of the two young men who were ardent enough, in a difficult time, to study the map to such good purpose. As Donne exclaimed: "Pictures in their eyes to get, was all their propagation." The pictures they chose may be different from some yourself might have taken; that is of course, for the field is endless. Their pilgrimage was, in the English phrase that used sometimes to annoy us, "an American kind of thing to do." It was enormously worth doing if it reminds the mere verbalist that even the most far-travelled fancies had circumstance and local habitation.

Men's lingering thoughts can put strangeness upon the actual; place and feeling make the mutual courtesy of art. The picture herein of the two swans reminds me of a summer dusk when a friend and I loitered by the old stone bridge at Henley on the Thames. Four swans were coming downstream; they spread apart, apparently in practised calculation, and slid with cotillion timing each through one of the four low arches—like four lines of a perfect quatrain. Not Shakespeare nor Shenstone could have patterned it better. Sometimes it seems that even earth and creatures have been unlawfully aware. You can quote climate and geography and food and fog and still not explain it all. Unless you are foreign, of course you will never struggle to explain it; but to a visitor the comedy and the queerness will always occur. So it is Conrad the Pole, or James Bone and Macdonell, Scotsmen, or Brogan, Scotch-Erse or Capek the Czech, or Santayana the don who is really a Don, who bespeak England best in recent prose, so far as prose can measure. What the Royal Navy calls the Western Approaches are more likely to be baffled. What is the simple Yank to think of a nation whose prime minister is so evidently part bulldog and part elf? Is it not sensationally odd that one of the most perceiving (and foreboding) tributes to British character was in Hitler's *Mein Kampf?* The instant you begin to get heavily sentimental about Britain she will grieve you by some sturdy sardonic rebuff. Beware of supposing, from glimpses of antique renown, that she is minded only toward the Past. No people in history has thought harder of shapes to come.

*   *   *

The shabbiest sentimentality is to be ashamed of honest emotion toward things of noble memory. In the book of living are many passages that were marked by pleased or startled readers; the pages of England have been ticked in every margin by centuries of notation. Since we quoted Hazlitt's walk from Farnham to Alton (about ten miles), what else might he have seen in that neighborhood? Let's get out the map of Surrey (with a little bit of Hampshire) and have a look. If he had gone in the other direction, toward Guildford, he might have made a detour past Waverley Abbey, for which Scott's novels were named; and Moor Park, where Swift met Stella. Or, on the road to Alton, the first fork to the left would have brought him to White's Selborne, and Woolmer Pond where "some young men went down to hunt flappers." (This amused the boys of my generation; but flappers meant wild duck.) A few minutes' walk beyond Alton and he could have had his coffee—or tea, more likely —with Jane Austen. The same length of walk to the north would have reached Eversley, where a future rector would write *The Water Babies* and *Westward Ho.* A few miles to the south, across the gorse of Hankley Common, was Hindhead where *The Hound of the Baskervilles* was getting ready to be written a hundred years later. If he had stayed in Farnham he could have had his coffee, eventually, in the house where Cobbett was born. All these social possibilities in a few square inches of map taken at random.

No wonder we look with bifocal eyes on our envoys' glimpses where time and space are merging traffic. Was it behind one of these windows that Keats wrote to Fanny Brawne about spilling the currant jelly on his friend's *Ben Jonson?* Will the Bile Beans (see Piccadilly Circus) really keep us Happy and Slim, and Wrigley's give us "Vigour"? And there's an awning marked "S & G for tobaccos"—Good old Salmon & Gluckstein! There if anywhere you might find a copy of Sherlock Holmes's monograph, *Upon the Distinction Between the Ashes of the Various Tobaccos.* On Wimpole Street we see by the sign that the Barretts lived only seven doors from the corner of Weymouth Street. Was it round that corner Robert Browning had the carriage waiting? There seems to be a car parked at the wrong "kerb." By the lie of the shadows we guess the camera was looking south and the picture taken in the forenoon. I study these pictures as if I had taken them myself for that imagined boyish textbook. I remember when I first thought of it, sitting on the graveyard wall at Edmonton, trying to do a pencil sketch of the church where Charles Lamb is buried. Like all healthy young men I was great on graveyards in those days: Stoke Poges, of course; and an easy bike ride from there was Jordans for William Penn, and Beaconsfield for Edmund Waller who girdled a woman's waist with the prettiest verses ever written. Or it might be Old Fitz near Woodbridge, with the Persian rose by the stone; or that tablet at Stanton Harcourt to the lovers killed by lightning while embraced in a haystack. Pope wrote their epitaph (he always approved couplets) but it was thought too sprightly.

Student pilgrimages were not all so obviously romantic. I was equally thrilled by a country railway platform in Suffolk where a meeting with a professor turned young Stevenson's ambition toward writing; or the brook at Ashbourne in Derbyshire where Bozzy found Dr. Johnson trying to pole the dead cat over the dam. "This may be laughed at," says Boswell, "as too trifling to record." But in the margins of literature nothing is trifling. My friend Mifflin and I had cycled to Ashbourne (in the unreplaceable year 1911) as much on Izaak Walton's trail as on Dr. Johnson's. I think Walton caught more trout in Dove Dale than in the Itchen which our editors illustrate here. Rolling in summer sunset into the limestone hills of the Peak how surprised we were to find a signpost pointing "To Haddon Hall." Simple Philadelphians, we had thought that was only a hotel in Atlantic City. We even pushed our bikes up 1690 feet to the Cat and Fiddle, the loftiest pub in England. If these explorers some day give us a sequel (and I hope they will) I beg for a picture of Dove Dale, where Dr. Johnson found the scenery for his Happy Valley in *Rasselas*.

So one is tempted to jot down further imaginary visit and search. Lulworth Cove, on the coast of Dorset, where the *Maria Crowther* lay offshore and Keats saw the bright steadfast star of the Last Sonnet—Blake's cottage at Felpham where he conversed with Homer, Dante and Milton on the beach, even as Walt Whitman did at Coney Island—or the lovely old twi-gabled church at Dean Prior where Rev. Robert Herrick preached and then walked home for Sunday dinner with Prew, the maid, and Tracey, the spaniel. Or my own secret unaccomplished pilgrimage to the parishes I once spotted on the map of Norfolk: Great and Little Snoring. Imagine, to be vicar of Great Snoring...I said once "I'll never see those old places now," and a young woman replied with memorable enigma: "Don't worry, you always carry your own ruins with you."

I didn't mean to get so far off the beam, but this book sends the mind on curves. I was trying to think about the Sense of Place. Only from that humble footing, companionship with things of sight and touch, can the mind rise to larger vantage. The Place may be anywhere and happens by chance. The liveliness of what they now call Regional literatures in the U. S. shows the growth of that sense of actual surrounding. In my own case it happens that Tintagel means less to me than Hoboken; Riverside Drive is quite as thrilling as Plymouth Hoe, and some scrubby woods on Long Island as truly haunted as Windsor Forest. That must be privately so for all. Any place is dear where a human mind rose above the joy and torture of the flesh and said its triumphant word—

> *When artists bend their dreams and hands*
> *All ages with one key unlock,*
> *And Master Shakespeare's yellow sands*
> *Are on the shores of Paumanok.*

LIST OF CONTENTS

✳✳✳

LITERARY ENGLAND

Photographs by David E. Scherman and

Descriptive Text by Richard Wilcox

THE CASTLE AT TINTAGEL

*According to legend, here at Tintagel Castle in Cornwall,
King Arthur was born, and here lie buried
Tristan and Iseult.*

The Arthurian legend is one of the oldest English stories, telling of a king who saved his country, nurtured its chivalry, and fell through treachery, but who still lives in the fabled isle of Avalon from which he will return some day to resume his kingdom. The origins of the legend are lost in antiquity, but many English writers, notably Geoffrey of Monmouth, Sir Thomas Malory, and Alfred Tennyson, have immortalized Arthur and his Knights of the Round Table. Arthur was supposedly born at Tintagel Castle, and his ghost is said to haunt its bird-frequented ruins. At Tintagel too, lie buried Tristan and Iseult, where a vine and a rosebush over their graves intertwine to unite forever the ill-starred lovers.

Alfred Tennyson: THE COMING OF ARTHUR

Sir, for ye know that in King Uther's time
The prince and warrior Gorlois, he that held
Tintagil castle by the Cornish sea,
. . . And that same night, the night of the new year,
By reason of the bitterness and grief
That vext his mother, all before his time
Was Arthur born, and all as soon as born
Delivered at a secret postern-gate
To Merlin, to be holden far apart
Until his hour should come.

TINTAGEL CASTLE WAS THE BIRTHPLACE OF KING ARTHUR

WINCHESTER

A city in Hampshire is associated with Camelot,
the citadel of Arthur and the home of the
Knights of the Round Table

Sir Thomas Malory identified Winchester with Camelot, built
for Arthur and his court by the wizard Merlin. Whether
Camelot or not, Winchester was certainly a community of the
Britons, a Roman town, and the capital of the Saxon kingdom
of Wessex. Alfred the Great, Canute and William the Conqueror all used it as their seat of government. Beyond the far
right background of the picture is the Great Hall (one of the
few remains of the old castle), in which hangs a painting of
the Round Table, dating from the sixteenth century. The
cathedral, dedicated to St. Peter, St. Paul and the Holy Trinity,
is the most conspicuous building in the picture. Except for
St. Peter's at Rome it is the longest church in Europe — 560
feet. It preceded Westminster Abbey as the place of corona-
tion for English sovereigns.

* 2 *

Alfred Tennyson: THE HOLY GRAIL

O brother, had you known our mighty hall,
Which Merlin built for Arthur long ago!
For all the sacred mount of Camelot,
And all the dim rich city, roof by roof,
Tower after tower, spire beyond spire,
By grove, and garden-lawn, and rushing brook,
Climbs to the mighty hall that Merlin built.

WINCHESTER, AN ANCIENT CITY, WAS ARTHUR'S CAMELOT

* 3 *

THE BLOOD SPRING, GLASTONBURY

According to Arthurian legend, the Holy Grail, the cup from which Christ drank at the Last Supper, was buried here by Joseph of Arimathea. It was found by Sir Galahad.

Glastonbury, in Somerset, is the holiest spot in England. It was a center of Druid worship and here Joseph of Arimathea founded the first church in England. Here, says Arthurian legend, he brought the Holy Grail, in which he had caught the blood of the crucified Christ, and buried it where the Blood Spring now wells up. Arthur's Round Table vowed to seek for the Holy Grail, but Galahad was the only knight whose purity allowed him to find it. Joseph is supposed to have thrust his staff into the ground, and it grew into an enormous thorn tree which blossomed every year at Christmas. Puritans cut down the tree in the seventeenth century, but offshoots of it still grow at Glastonbury. The trunk behind the boys in the picture is believed to be one of them.

* 3 *

Alfred Tennyson: THE HOLY GRAIL

The cup, the cup itself, from which our Lord
Drank at the last sad supper with his own.
This, from the blessed land of Aromat—
After the day of darkness, when the dead
Went wandering o'er Moriah—the good saint
Arimathaean Joseph, journeying brought
To Glastonbury, where the winter thorn
Blossoms at Christmas, mindful of our Lord.
And there awhile it bode;

THE BLOOD SPRING MARKS WHERE THE HOLY GRAIL WAS BURIED

✳ 4 ✳

DOZMARY POOL

When Arthur was gravely wounded, Sir Bedivere threw
Excalibur, the King's fabulous sword, into
this lake on Cornwall's Bodmin Moor.

Dozmary Pool is a small, rush-bordered lake on lonely Bodmin Moor, near Camelford, supposedly the place where Arthur was wounded in his last battle. He told Sir Bedivere, who had carried him from the field, to throw his sword into the pool. Bedivere twice refrained, attracted by the richness of its jewels, but he finally cast it into the waters. The arm of the Lady of the Lake, clothed in white samite, caught Excalibur, flourished it three times, then drew it below the surface.

* 4 *

Sir Thomas Malory: MORTE D'ARTHUR

"Therefore," said Arthur unto Sir Bedivere, "take thou Excalibur my good sword and go with it to yonder water side, and when thou comest there I charge thee throw my sword in that water, and come again and tell me what thou there seest."

LEGENDS SAY EXCALIBUR WAS THROWN INTO DOZMARY POOL

* 5 *

THE ABBEY AT GLASTONBURY

*Founded by Joseph of Arimathea, it is an impressive
medieval ruin. Here Sir Bedivere dwelt as
a hermit after Arthur's death.*

Glastonbury Abbey was untouched by the battles of conquest
in England and remained to link early and late Christianity in
the island. Said to have been founded either in the second or
third century, Glastonbury Abbey flourished uninterruptedly
until the time of Henry VIII, who hanged the last abbot. De-
spoiled of their valuable contents, the buildings were there-
after neglected and were even used as a stone quarry. Some
legends say that Arthur and Guinevere were buried here in
adjoining tombs.

Sir Thomas Malory: MORTE D'ARTHUR

Yet some men say in many parts of England that King Arthur is not dead, but had by the will of our Lord Jesu into another place; and men say that he shall come again, and he shall win the holy cross. I will not say it shall be so, but rather I will say, here in this world he changed his life. But many men say that there is written upon his tomb this verse: HIC JACET ARTHURUS, REX QUONDAM, REXQUE FUTURUS. Thus leave I here Sir Bedivere with the hermit, that dwelled that time in a chapel beside Glastonbury, and there was his hermitage. And so they lived in their prayers and fastings, and great abstinence.

GLASTONBURY ABBEY IS NOW IN RUINS

* 6 *

THE ISLE OF ATHELNEY

*In the marshes of Somerset, King Alfred hid from the
conquering Danes. During the ninth century
he revived learning in western England.*

The Isle of Athelney is a marshy region to which Alfred retired
when he was defeated by the Danes. Here, legend has it, a
peasant woman who did not know his station had him watch
the cakes she was baking. Thinking of his misfortunes, the
monarch forgot the cakes, which were burned when the good-
wife returned, so that she railed at him for his neglect. Though
it is popularly supposed that he was a fugitive at Athelney,
Alfred actually had a part of his army there and kept fighting
his country's invaders. Successful in battle, he continued to
encourage the restoration of culture in his kingdom of Wessex.
The Anglo-Saxon Chronicle, a chronology of events in England compiled by monks, is typical of the literary efforts he
fostered. It is thought that Alfred himself may have written
parts of the *Chronicle*.

* 6 *

ANGLO-SAXON CHRONICLE

. . . and most of the people they reduced except the King Alfred, and he with a little band made his way . . . by wood and swamp, and after Easter he . . . made a fort at Athelney, and from that fort kept fighting against the foe.

A STONE MONUMENT MARKS THE SPOT WHERE ALFRED HID FROM THE DANES

7

THE MALVERN HILLS

These are the hills that sheltered William Langland,
who called himself "Long Will" and wrote
the allegorical poem Piers Plowman.

Except for Chaucer's *Canterbury Tales*, the greatest work in Middle English is William Langland's *The Vision of William Concerning Piers the Plowman*. There are three versions of this long alliterative poem, all abounding in allegorical figures and vivid descriptions of contemporary English life. They were immensely popular throughout the latter fourteenth and the entire fifteenth and sixteenth centuries. The fact that about sixty manuscripts still survive testifies to their wide appeal, though no version was printed until 1550. Their authorship has been much disputed, but it seems most probable that William Langland actually did write *Piers Plowman*. Little is known of Langland himself except that he was well acquainted with the western midlands and London.

∗ 7 ∗

William Langland: PIERS, THE PLOWMAN

In a summer season, when soft was the sun,
I clad me in rough clothing, a shepherd as I were;
In habit of hermit, unholy of works,
Went I wide in this world, wonders to hear.
But on a May morning in the Malverne Hills
To me befell a marvel, a fairy thing methought.

THE MALVERN HILLS ARE PLEASANT UNDER THE LATE SPRING SUN

* 8 *

CANTERBURY CATHEDRAL

The pilgrims of Chaucer's day saw the great church from the road that topped the Kentish hills. Their stories are told in The Canterbury Tales.

The cathedral church of the Primate of All England rises over the old walled town of Canterbury and overlooks the hop fields of Kent. Until Henry VIII's time, it held the shrine of the murdered archbishop, St. Thomas à Becket, to which the pious traveled along the Pilgrims' Way from Winchester, while other devotees streamed down from London along the old Roman road called Watling Street. In Chaucer's *Canterbury Tales* a group of these pilgrims tell stories to keep themselves amused during the trip from London. Chaucer, usually considered the father of English literature, was England's greatest medieval poet. *The Canterbury Tales* is his masterpiece.

Geoffrey Chaucer: CANTERBURY TALES

Whan that Aprille with his shoures soote

The droghte of March hath perced to the roote . . .

Than longen folk to goon on pilgrimages. . . .

And specially from every shires ende

Of Engelond to Caunterbury they wende,

The holy blisful martir for to seke,

That hem hath holpen, whan that they were seke.

THIS WAS THE PILGRIMS' FIRST SIGHT OF CANTERBURY CATHEDRAL

* 9 *

BERRY POMEROY CASTLE

The home of the Seymours, who gave England
a queen, is a stone pile set in the
green fields of Devonshire.

Jane Seymour, Henry VIII's third wife, never lived at Berry
Pomeroy. She was lucky enough to give England a male heir,
and the Seymours profited. Although Jane reigned only a
year before her death, her father became the greatest man in
England when his small grandson, Edward VI, became king.
He also became the greatest land-grabber, and in a shady real
estate deal the Pomeroys' ancestral acres somehow passed to
the Seymours. To the old buildings they added a Tudor man-
sion so large that "it was a good day's work for a servant but
to open and shut the casements." Fired by lightning, Berry
Pomeroy has been desolate for two centuries, but Queen Jane,
demure architect of her family's larger fortunes, still lives in an
old ballad.

SIXTEENTH-CENTURY BALLAD

Whenas King Henry ruled this land
He had a Queen, I understand
Lord Seymour's daughter, fair and bright;
Yet death by his remorseless power
Did blast the bloom of this fair flower;
O mourn, mourn, mourn, fair ladies,
Your Queen the flower of England's dead.

BERRY POMEROY CASTLE WAS BEGUN IN THE THIRTEENTH CENTURY

* 10 *

SWANS ON THE THAMES

Edmund Spenser's Prothalamion *is an allegorical poem of
two sisters who, as swans, descend the Thames
to London for their bridal day.*

The Thames, the principal river of England, rises in Gloucestershire on a slope of the Cotswold hills. It bounds part of the counties of Gloucester, Oxford, Buckingham, Middlesex, Essex, Wiltshire, Berkshire, Surrey and Kent, and flows through London. Many are its associations with English literature. Edmund Spenser, for instance, invoked the Thames in his beautiful *Prothalamion*, "a spousall verse" written to celebrate the double marriage of Ladies Elizabeth and Katherine Somerset, daughters of the Earl of Somerset. Spenser was the first major English poet to follow Chaucer, who had died two centuries before. His great work, *The Faerie Queene*, was written to glorify England and its "most royal Queen," Elizabeth.

10

Edmund Spenser: PROTHALAMION

With that I saw two Swannes of goodly hewe
Come softly swimming downe along the Lee;
Two fairer Birds I yet did never see;
The snow, which doth the top of Pindus strew,
Did never whiter shew;
Nor Jove himselfe, when he a Swan would be
For love of Leda, whiter did appeare;
Yet Leda, was (they say) as white as he,
Yet not so white as these, nor nothing neare;
So purely white they were,
That even the gentle streame, the which them bare,
Seem'd foule to them, and bad his billowes spare
To wet their fayre plumes with water not so fayre,
And marre their beauties bright,
That shone as heavens light,
Against their Brydale day, which was not long:
Sweete Themmes! runne softly, till I end my Song.

TWO SWANS GLIDE DOWN THE THAMES TOWARDS LONDON

11

THE ENGLISH COAST

It typified the invulnerability of England to her greatest and most devoted writer, William Shakespeare.

The highest place in English literature belongs to William Shakespeare. Born in 1564 at Stratford on Avon, in Warwickshire, he died there in 1616. He spent most of his life in London, where he wrote the plays and sonnets that are part of the heritage of all English-speaking peoples. Of all her writers, he loved most the soil, the associations, and the history of his native land. The picture shows a section of the Cornish coast, where the bleak and jagged shore "spurns back the ocean's roaring tides."

* ‖ *

William Shakespeare: KING RICHARD II

This fortress built by nature for herself

Against infection and the hand of war,

This happy breed of men, this little world,

This precious stone set in the silver sea,

Which serves it in the office of a wall

Or as a moat defensive to a house,

Against the envy of less happier lands,

This blessed plot, this earth, this realm,

    this England.

THE COASTS OF ENGLAND WERE THE RAMPARTS OF SHAKESPEARE'S WORLD

∗ 12 ∗

LOVERS IN WARWICKSHIRE

*A boy and a girl like them inspired
one of William Shakespeare's
finest lyrics.*

Shakespeare's plays are interspersed with lovely lyrics, many of them songs of the country that he had known as a boy and young man in the fields of Warwickshire, near Stratford. Warwickshire is as green as ever, and lovers still walk in the fields, just as they did in the sixteenth century.

12

William Shakespeare: AS YOU LIKE IT

It was a lover and his lass,
　　With a hey, and a ho, and a hey nonino,
That o'er the green corn-field did pass,
　　In the spring time, the only pretty ring time,
When birds do sing, hey ding a ding, ding:
Sweet lovers love the spring.

A BOY AND A GIRL WALK THROUGH THE COUNTRY NEAR STRATFORD

13

GREENWAY HOUSE

*It was the home of Humphrey Gilbert and Walter Raleigh,
two Elizabethans who helped discover
and colonize the New World.*

Greenway House, in which Sir Humphrey Gilbert was born
and his half brother, Sir Walter Raleigh, lived, stands on a hill
in Devon overlooking the river Dart. Both were famous explorers in the days of Elizabeth, when England was wresting
control of the seas from Spain. Gilbert established in New-
foundland the first English colony in America, and Raleigh
helped settle Virginia. Raleigh, who was also a poet, was ex-
ecuted in 1618. Accounts of both their voyages are found in
Richard Hakluyt's monumental *Principall Navigations, Voi-
agaes, and Discoveries of the English Nation*, the book on
which Hakluyt spent most of his life. Sir Francis Drake, who
recruited the seamen who met and defeated the Spanish
Armada, was born a little more than twenty miles away from
Greenway House.

* | 3 *

Richard Hakluyt: PRINCIPALL NAVIGATIONS, VOIAGES, & DISCOVERIES OF THE ENGLISH NATION

On Thursday the 6. of February in the yere 1595.
we departed England, and the Sunday following
had sight of the North cape of Spaine, the winde
for the most part continuing prosperous:

[Journal of Sir Walter Raleigh]

A fourth way to go unto these aforesaid happy
Islands Moluccae sir Humphrey Gilbert a learned
and valiant knight discourseth of at large in his
new passage to Cathayo.

GREENWAY HOUSE IS IN THE HEART OF THE RALEIGH COUNTRY

* 14 *

THE ITCHEN RIVER

*Izaak Walton, a happy man, dreamed and fished along
English country streams. He died at Winchester,
on the banks of the Itchen River.*

The Compleat Angler is a book beloved by many who are not
interested in fishing. It is a book about cheerful men who enjoy
the simple pleasures of the country. Starting as a dialogue
between a fisherman, a hunter and a fowler, it goes on to tell
how best to catch and prepare fresh-water fish, how to tie flies,
and which streams are the best for trout and grayling. Walton
also wrote *Lives* of Donne, George Herbert and other contem-
poraries, and these are touched with the same quiet humor and
honesty as his more famous work. The latter part of his life was
spent in the city of Winchester, near which he angled in the
tiny Itchen River.

Izaak Walton: COMPLEAT ANGLER

No life, my honest scholar, no life so happy and so pleasant as the life of a well governed angler; for when the lawyer is swallowed up with business and the statesman is preventing or contriving plots, then we sit on cowslip banks, hear the birds sing and possess ourselves in as much quietness as these silent silver streams which we now see glide so quietly by us. God never did make a more calm, quiet, innocent recreation than angling.

TWO BOYS FISH IN THE ITCHEN, ONCE LOVED BY IZAAK WALTON

A HILL AT HORTON

John Milton may have trod this very hill
while composing Lycidas in memory
of his friend, Edward King.

After John Milton left Christ's College, Cambridge, he lived for five years with his father at Horton, in Buckinghamshire. It was here that he wrote the two beautiful poems in contrasting moods, *L'Allegro* and *Il Penseroso*, and what is perhaps the greatest elegy in all English literature, *Lycidas*, in memory of his friend, Edward King, who had drowned in the Irish Sea. *Lycidas* sounds the first majestic notes that Milton was to develop symphonically in *Paradise Lost*. As learned in Latin as in his native tongue, Milton later served as secretary to Oliver Cromwell's Council of State. While holding this office he became blind, and despite this handicap he composed those great religious epics which have placed their author among the most sublime of all English poets.

* 15 *

John Milton: "LYCIDAS"

For we were nursed upon the self-same hill,
Fed the same flock by fountain, shade, and rill.
Together both, ere the high lawns appear'd
Under the opening eye-lids of the Morn,
We drove a-field, and both together heard
What time the gray-fly winds her sultry horn,
Battening our flocks with the fresh dews of night;
Oft till the star, that rose at evening bright,
Towards heaven's descent had sloped his westering wheel.

MILTON WALKED AMONG THE HILLS OF HORTON

* 16 *

ST. CLEMENT DANES, IN THE STRAND

*The lovely steepled church where Samuel Johnson
worshiped was gutted by flames
during the bombing of London.*

London is a city of beautiful churches, and the bells in their spires, speaking to one another across the roofs, became a nursery rhyme known to all English children. "The bells of St. Martin's," in St. Martin's-le-Grand, and the "great bell at Bow" had each their own sayings, but the soft, silvery notes of St. Clement's said "oranges and lemons." The bells were melted in the fire that destroyed the church.

* 16 *

OLD ENGLISH NURSERY RHYME

Gay go up and gay go down
To ring the bells of London town:
"Oranges and lemons"
Say the bells of St. Clement's.

ONLY THE WALLS AND SPIRE REMAIN OF ST. CLEMENT'S, IN THE STRAND

∗ 17 ∗

BATTLE ABBEY

*Thomas Chatterton, "the marvelous boy," wrote
of this spot where Harold fell and William
gained the throne of England.*

In the year 1066, William the Conqueror, a Norman, met the
Saxon Harold's armies on the heights of Senlac, north of Hast-
ings. He vowed to build an abbey if he was successful, and today a monument a few yards to the right of the Abbey marks the
place where Harold fell, mortally wounded. Thomas Chatterton devoted one of his "Rowley poems" to the battle of Hast-
ings. These were the poems that Chatterton offered to the
public as the work of a fifteenth-century Bristol monk, but the
forgeries were soon exposed. In 1770 he went to London, where
his burlesque opera, *The Revenge*, was successfully produced.
But the young poet was destitute and, in despair, he poisoned
himself. He died in a garret at the age of seventeen.

17

Thomas Chatterton: THE BATTLE OF HASTINGS

O Chryste, it is a grief for me to telle,
How manie a nobil erle and valrous knyghte
In fyghtynge for Kynge Harrold noblie fell,
Al sleyne in Hastyngs feeld in bloudie fyghte.

THE RUINS OF BATTLE ABBEY COMMEMORATE WILLIAM'S VICTORY

18

BURRINGTON GORGE

Seeking shelter from a sudden thunderstorm,
Augustus Montague Toplady here composed
his immortal hymn, Rock of Ages.

The "*Rock of Ages*" and the cleft in the rock are not merely symbolic phrases. There actually is a great rock in Burrington Gorge, near Burrington in Somersetshire, where the composer of the hymn by that name hid one day from a thunderstorm. Augustus Montague Toplady, an eighteenth-century clergyman who was the incumbent of a small church near Burrington, was walking through the gorge when the storm came up. Crouching in the cleft of the rock to escape the sudden downpour, he was moved to write the hymn that was to become one of the most famous in our language. Such, at least, is the persistent legend which deserves to be true.

✳ 18 ✳

Augustus Toplady: ROCK OF AGES

Rock of ages, cleft for me,

Let me hide myself in thee.

Let the water and the blood

From thy riven side which flow'd

Be of sin the double cure,

Cleanse me from its guilt and power.

AUGUSTUS TOPLADY SHELTERED IN THE ROCK OF AGES' CLEFT

STOKE POGES CHURCHYARD

Thomas Gray is buried in the same Buckinghamshire church-
yard that he described in his Elegy. It is still a place
of old trees and grass-covered graves.

Thomas Gray's *Elegy Written in a Country Churchyard* was
inspired by the little church at Stoke Poges where he used to go
while visiting his widowed mother who lived in the village. In
1750 he sent the poem to Horace Walpole with whom he had
become reconciled after a quarrel. Described by the poet as "a
thing with an end to it," the *Elegy* is one of the most beloved
works in English literature. In 1757 Gray was offered the post
of Poet Laureate, in succession to Colley Cibber, but refused
to accept it. Eleven years later he became a Cambridge don. He
was buried in 1771, near his mother, in the churchyard he loved
so well.

Thomas Gray: ELEGY WRITTEN IN A COUNTRY CHURCHYARD

Beneath those rugged elms, that yew-tree's shade,
Where heaves the turf in many a mould'ring heap,
Each in his narrow cell for ever laid,
The rude forefathers of the hamlet sleep.

• • •

Some village-Hampden, that with dauntless breast
The little tyrant of his fields withstood;
Some mute inglorious Milton here may rest,
Some Cromwell, guiltless of his country's blood.

THOMAS GRAY'S GRAVE LIES UNDER THE TREES TO THE LEFT

* 20 *

FLEET STREET

*Today the center of English journalism, it was
once the haunt of Samuel Johnson and
his biographer, Boswell.*

Fleet Street, now the home of many London newspapers, was
once known as "tipling street," because of its many tavern
signs. But long before the days of modern newspapers, it was
associated with authors and book publishers. Near this street
lived Samuel Johnson, the literary dictator of his age, and many
of the conversations recorded by his faithful biographer, James
Boswell, took place in its old taverns and coffeehouses.

* 20 *

James Boswell: LIFE OF SAMUEL JOHNSON

It was a delightful day: as we walked to St. Clement's Church, I again remarked that Fleet Street was the most cheerful scene in the world. "Fleet Street," said I, "is in my mind more delightful than Tempé." JOHNSON. "Ay, sir, but let it be compared with Mull."

AT ONE END, FLEET STREET LOOKS TO THE DOME OF ST. PAUL'S

THE PASS AT KIRKSTONE

Where the Roman general, Agricola, led one of his columns
into Westmoreland, three English poets
loved to wander.

The beautiful mountains and lakes of Cumberland and West-moreland are closely associated with a notable school of English poetry—the Lake School—comprising William Wordsworth, Samuel Taylor Coleridge and Robert Southey. Although none of these mountains is very high, or the lakes very long, their picturesqueness and wildness are marked. Wordsworth, in particular, made the district his own, and few points of interest are left unsung in his long poem, *Excursion*, or in a number of his minor poems.

❋ 21 ❋

William Wordsworth: THE PASS AT KIRKSTONE

Within the mind strong fancies work.

A deep delight the bosom thrills

Oft as I pass along the fork

Of these fraternal hills:

Where, save the rugged road, we find

No appanage of human kind,

Nor hint of man . . .

WORDSWORTH AND COLERIDGE OFTEN WALKED IN KIRKSTONE PASS

* 22 *

DAFFODILS AT ULLSWATER

The flowers that filled the poet's heart
with pleasure still grow at the edge
of an English lake.

One day early in spring William Wordsworth was taking his customary long walk through the Lake Country of Cumberland when suddenly he came upon a host of daffodils "tossing their heads in sprightly dance." "The daffodils," he wrote later, "grew and still grow on the margin of Ullswater, and probably may be seen to this day as beautiful in the month of March, nodding their golden heads beside the dancing and foaming waves." Wordsworth wrote these words over a hundred years ago, but the flowers in the picture still bloom every year where he first saw them on the banks of Ullswater Lake.

* 22 *

William Wordsworth: DAFFODILS

I wandered lonely as a cloud
That floats on high o'er vales and hills,
When all at once I saw a crowd,
A host, of golden daffodils;
Beside the lake, beneath the trees,
Fluttering and dancing in the breeze.

THE DAFFODILS AT ULLSWATER BROUGHT JOY TO WILLIAM WORDSWORTH

* 23 *

KEATS GROVE

*Here, in this house in Hampstead, now a suburb
of London, John Keats wrote many
of his greatest poems.*

Hyperion, *The Eve of St. Agnes, Ode to a Nightingale* and many other of Keats' matchless poems were written in this Hampstead house. In those days the house was divided into two, one part being occupied by Mrs. Brawne and her children, including Fanny with whom John Keats was passionately in love. During his last six weeks in England, John, seriously ill with tuberculosis, was nursed by Mrs. Brawne and Fanny in their part of the house. In September, 1820, he started on his last trip to Rome, where he died less than a year later, at the age of twenty-five.

* 23 *

John Keats: SONNET

When I have fears that I may cease to be
Before my pen has glean'd my teeming brain,
Before high-piled books, in charact'ry,
Hold like rich garners the full-ripen'd grain;
When I behold, upon the night's starr'd face,
Huge cloudy symbols of a high romance,
And feel that I may never live to trace
Their shadows, with the magic hand of chance;
And when I feel, fair creature of an hour!
That I shall never look upon thee more,
Never have relish in the faery power
Of unreflecting love;—then on the shore
  Of the wide world I stand alone, and think,
  Till Love and Fame to nothingness do sink.

THIS HAMPSTEAD HOUSE SHELTERED THE SORROW-LADEN KEATS

24

AN OAK IN SHERWOOD FOREST

*Here Robin Hood and his band of Merrie Men, dear
to the hearts of English folk from time
immemorial, had their hide-out.*

Robin Hood, famed in English ballad and story, may be a
legendary character, as historians claim, but he is very real to
the English people. He is a folk hero who lived with his outlaw
band in the forest, robbing the rich but always sparing the poor,
and allowing no woman ever to be molested. History knows
nothing of Robin Hood's supposed original, Robert Fitz-Ooth
of Nottinghamshire, who was reputed to have been Earl of
Huntingdon in the twelfth century. But Sherwood Forest, now
on the fringe of one of the world's richest coal-mining districts,
will forever be associated with Robin and Maid Marian, with
Friar Tuck, Little John and all his other merrie men.

John Keats: ROBIN HOOD

On the fairest time of June
You may go, with sun or moon,
Or the seven stars to light you,
Or the polar ray to right you;
But you never may behold
Little John, or Robin bold;
Never one, of all the clan,
Thrumming on an empty can
Some old hunting ditty, while
He doth his green way beguile
To fair hostess Merriment,
Down beside the pasture Trent;
For he left the merry tale
Messenger for spicy ale.

ROBIN HOOD LIVED AMONG THE OAKS OF SHERWOOD FOREST

THE ROYAL PAVILION AT BRIGHTON

*George IV called it home. It was built for him in the
early nineteenth century, the period Thackeray
wrote about in Vanity Fair.*

Brighton, a famous seaside resort in Sussex, was popular before
the Prince of Wales—George IV to be—made it fashionable as
well. He began taking his holidays here with the lovely Mrs.
Fitzherbert, whom he later married. Brighton became his pet
fad, and he finally built the fantastic Royal Pavilion in which
to hold dances and entertain his friends. Few buildings have
caused more violent comment, and it is itself a comment on
the taste of the man who was called the First Gentleman of
Europe. Readers of *Vanity Fair* will remember that Becky
Sharp, Amelia Sedley, and their husbands come to Brighton
before embarking for the Continent—and Waterloo. Thackeray's description of Brighton still holds: it is, if anything, more
motley than ever, as its nickname, "London by the Sea,"
implies.

William Makepeace Thackeray: VANITY FAIR

. . . But have we any leisure for a description of Brighton?—for Brighton, a clean Naples with genteel lazzaroni; for Brighton, that always looks brisk, gay, and gaudy, like a harlequin's jacket; for Brighton, which used to be seven hours distant from London at the time of our story, which is now only a hundred minutes off, and which may approach who knows how much nearer, unless Joinville comes and untimely bombards it.

THE PAVILION AT BRIGHTON WAS ONCE A ROYAL RESIDENCE

* 26 *

DICKENS' HOUSE

*Betsey Trotwood, David Copperfield's aunt, lived in a house
like this one at Broadstairs, where her creator,
Charles Dickens, spent several seasons.*

When David Copperfield could no longer stand his life of
poverty and wretchedness in London, he walked to Dover to
see whether his aunt could help him out. He found her living
in a house such as the one in the picture, and here he began
to realize that life can be a joy. A house on the Parade, at
Broadstairs, is believed to have furnished the model for Betsey
Trotwood's. This is very likely, for Broadstairs is also on the
Kentish coast, about twenty-five miles from Dover. One does
not need a very profound understanding of Dickens to know
that all his experiences had to do double duty—in his own life
and in his novels. In this case, the charming but not unusual
house at Broadstairs seems invested with more charm—and
positive uniqueness—when changed by Dickens' powerful
magic into Betsey Trotwood's home.

* 26 *

Charles Dickens: DAVID COPPERFIELD

"This is Miss Trotwood's," said the young woman. "Now you know; and that's all I have got to say." With which words she hurried into the house, as if to shake off the responsibility of my appearance; and left me standing at the garden-gate, looking disconsolately over the top of it towards the parlor-window, where a muslin curtain partly undrawn in the middle, a large round green screen or fan fastened on to the window-sill, a small table, and a great chair, suggested to me that my aunt might be at that moment seated in awful state.

DICKENS' HOUSE AT BROADSTAIRS WAS BETSEY TROTWOOD'S HOME

THE ASSEMBLY ROOMS AT BATH

Dickens' Mr. Pickwick attended a ball and played whist
at the Assembly Rooms. They were ruined
during a German "Baedeker raid."

When Mr. Samuel Pickwick had unsuccessfully contested a breach-of-promise suit brought against him by Mrs. Bardell, his landlady, he felt in need of a holiday. This—despite the damages of £750 awarded to the plaintiff—he took rather lavishly at Bath. At the Assembly Rooms, called by students of architecture the finest of their kind in Europe, he went to a ball and sat down to whist with three formidable old ladies. Nor did he leave Bath without other adventures of a more incredible—and Pickwickian—sort. Dickens modeled his most lovable and popular character on a real person. This was a certain John Foster, "a fat old beau" who wore "drab tights and black gaiters."

Charles Dickens: PICKWICK PAPERS

... In the ball-room, the long card-room, the octagonal card-room, the staircases, and the passages, the hum of many voices, and the sound of many feet, were perfectly bewildering. Dresses rustled, feathers waved, lights shone, and jewels sparkled. There was the music—not of the quadrille band, for it had not yet commenced; but the music of soft tiny footsteps, with now and then a clear merry laugh—low and gentle, but very pleasant to hear in a female voice, whether in Bath or elsewhere. Brilliant eyes, lighted up with pleasurable expectation, gleamed from every side; and look where you would, some exquisite form glided gracefully through the throng, and was no sooner lost, than it was replaced by another as dainty and bewitching.

PICKWICK WATCHED A BALL IN THE NOW FIRE-BLACKENED ASSEMBLY ROOMS AT BATH

* 28 *

A LONDON SHOP

*Little Nell may have waited on trade in this musty old building
in Portsmouth Street. Every sentimental pilgrimage to
London includes the Old Curiosity Shop.*

Push open the door of No. 14 Portsmouth Street, and be carried back a hundred years. It is almost hard to believe that Little Nell does not bob up to take your order (though this is a browsing type of shop). And where is Grandfather Trent, doting, foolish, but lovable old man? This picturesque old place, perhaps built in the days of Queen Bess, has been so long associated with the characters in Dickens' *The Old Curiosity Shop* that it is something of a shock not to find them present as solid flesh and blood.

* 28 *

Charles Dickens: THE OLD CURIOSITY SHOP

The place through which he made his way at leisure was one of those receptacles for old and curious things which seem to crouch in odd corners of this town and to hide their musty treasures from the public eye in jealousy and distrust.

LITTLE NELL LIVED IN THE OLD CURIOSITY SHOP

* 29 *

BATH

*Its hot springs are its fortune. The Romans built magnificent
baths here, and since then it has often been a
center of fashion and gaiety.*

The mineral waters of Bath are the only hot springs in England. Around them the Romans built a fabulous city of pleasure. Fashionable Bath passed with the Romans, and many hundred years went by before its fame returned. Early in the eighteenth century, Beau Nash, a gambler, became the arbiter of Bath society. For those lingering there for the cure—"taking the waters," it was called—he prescribed the simple code of dancing, cards and gossip. Many an English man of letters commented on this cult, not always admiringly. Landor rapturously called Bath "the Florence of England," and Jane Austen doted on it. She lived for a time in one of its calm Palladian houses, and her first novel, *Northanger Abbey*, is laid partly in Bath.

Jane Austen: NORTHANGER ABBEY

With more than usual eagerness did Catherine hasten to the Pump Room the next day, secure within herself of seeing Mr. Tilney there before the morning was over, and ready to meet him with a smile; but no smile was demanded—Mr. Tilney did not appear. Every creature in Bath, except himself, was to be seen in the Room at different periods of the fashionable hours; crowds of people were every moment passing in and out, up the steps and down; people whom nobody cared about, and nobody wanted to see; and he only was absent. "What a delightful place Bath is," said Mrs. Allen as they sat down near the great clock, after parading the Room till they were tired; "and how pleasant it would be if we had any acquaintances here."

THE ROMANS ONCE USED THE WARM SPRINGS AT BATH

* 30 *

NAWORTH CASTLE

This residence of the Earl of Carlisle looks more like a fortress
than a home. But its strong walls were needed when
"Belted" Will Howard held it against the Scots.

For centuries the history of England has been the history of
the Howards, her noblest family. Many a fierce battle was
fought between the northern Howards and the Scotch bor-
derers. Naworth Castle, where "Belted" Will held state, was
dangerously near the bloody line of demarcation between the
two kingdoms. This stern upholder of law and order was much
feared and respected by his neighbors, both English and
Scotch. They called him "Bold Willie," while his wife—a great
heiress who had brought many acres to Howard—was styled
"Bessie o' the braid [broad] apron." Sir Walter Scott, whose
ancestors had done their share of fighting against the Howards
of Naworth, immortalized "Belted" Will in *The Lay of the*
Last Minstrel.

* 30 *

Sir Walter Scott: THE LAY OF THE LAST MINSTREL

Why do these steeds stand ready dight?
Why watch these warriors, arm'd by night?—
They watch, to hear the blood-hound baying;
They watch, to hear the war horn braying;
To see St. George's red cross streaming,
To see the midnight beacon gleaming,
They watch, against southern force and guile,
Lest Scroop, or Howard, or Percy's powers,
Threaten Branksome's lordly towers,
From Warkworth, or Naworth, or merry Carlisle.

NAWORTH CASTLE IS ON THE SCOTCH BORDER

* 31 *

CLUN CASTLE

*Eight hundred years is old age even for a medieval
castle. Yet Clun might be intact today if it
had not been blown up in the Civil War.*

Literary associations cluster around Clun, one of the most
out-of-the-way towns in Shropshire. The castle, whose shell
rises over the village, was long a bulwark against the Welsh.
Sir Walter Scott portrayed it, as the Garde Doloureuse, in *The
Betrothed*. From it beautiful Eveline Berenger was rescued by
the Constable of Chester after her father had been killed in a
foray against the Welsh. For centuries the castle has belonged
to the Duke of Norfolk, who also bears the title of Baron Clun.
It lies in the *Shropshire Lad* country, and so has again become
a place of pilgrimage.

✳ 31 ✳

Sir Walter Scott: THE BETROTHED

A place strong by nature and well fortified by art, which the Welsh Prince had found it impossible to conquer either by open force or stratagem, and which, remaining with a strong garrison in his rear, often checked his invasions by rendering his retreat precarious.

CLUN CASTLE WAS AN ENGLISH OUTPOST AGAINST THE WELSH

* 32 *

TOP WITHENS

Emily Brontë wrote her strange novel, Wuthering Heights, about a farmhouse on the windy Yorkshire moors near which she lived with her gifted sisters.

Wuthering Heights was the only novel written by Emily Brontë, although she is considered by many to be the foremost of all English women writers. "My sister Emily loved the moors," Charlotte Brontë wrote. "Flowers brighter than the rose bloomed in the blackest of the heath for her—out of a sullen hollow in a livid hillside, her mind could make an Eden." To Emily, the old farmhouse, near Pennistone Crag, was beautiful, and she used it as the model for Cathy's on Wuthering Heights. Open to the northern blast, it seems to symbolize the austere passion that had proudly sung: "No coward soul is mine . . ."

Emily Brontë: WUTHERING HEIGHTS

Wuthering Heights is the name of Mr. Heathcliff's dwelling, "Wuthering" being a significant provincial adjective, descriptive of the atmospheric tumult to which its station is exposed in stormy weather. Pure, bracing ventilation they must have up there at all times, indeed; one may guess the power of the north wind blowing over the edge, by the excessive slant of a few stunted firs at the end of the house; and by a range of gaunt thorns all stretching their limbs one way, as if craving alms of the sun. Happily, the architect had foresight to build it strong; the narrow windows are deeply set in the wall, and the corners defended with large jutting stones.

HEATHCLIFF AND CATHY LIVED AS CHILDREN IN WUTHERING HEIGHTS

* 33 *

AN ENGLISH ELM

*In Italy Robert Browning longed for a sight
of English trees and hedgerows and
fields in early spring.*

Robert Browning loved many things—life, a good cause, his
wife and, with equal passion, Italy and England. In 1844, he
set forth on his third voyage to Italy, going by way of Naples.
Savoring that landscape of paradise, he proceeded north, and
at Leghorn visited Edward John Trelawny, who had witnessed
Shelley's death. This Italian trip flowered then and later in
many romances and lyrics, but none is more loved than *Home
Thoughts from Abroad*. Sick of "this gaudy melon flower,"
surfeited with the lushness of the Italian scene, in *Home-
Thoughts* he wrote of the hedgerows and wet green fields he
remembered from spring mornings in his own land.

Robert Browning: HOME-THOUGHTS FROM ABROAD

Oh, to be in England
Now that April's there,
And whoever wakes in England
Sees, some morning, unaware
That the lowest boughs and the brush-wood sheaf
Round the elm-bole are in tiny leaf,
While the chaffinch sings on the orchard bough
In England—now!

AN ENGLISH ELM AGAINST THE SKY AT DAWN

* 34 *

WIMPOLE STREET

A tyrannical father made No. 50 Wimpole Street a prison
for Elizabeth Barrett. She escaped by eloping
with her lover, Robert Browning.

As a young girl, Elizabeth Barrett suffered an accident which—her despotic father determined—would make her an incurable invalid. He kept her in a darkened room at their home in Wimpole Street (in the picture the seventh house from the right). Robert Browning, attracted by her verses, began a lengthy correspondence with the explosive "I love your books, and I love you too." Finally he visited her, and their friendship deepened into love. Browning, a man of action, persuaded Elizabeth to elope with him. She left her father's house on September 12, 1846, married Browning the same day, and went with him to Italy. Her father disowned her and refused to correspond with her. But paternal wrath had little effect on Elizabeth's idyl, and she poured forth her love for Robert in the tender, passionately felt *Sonnets from the Portuguese*.

* 34 *

Elizabeth Barrett Browning: LETTER TO HER SISTERS

I am going to write to Papa—and to George—
very soon, I shall . . . Dear George,—I love him to
his worth. And my poor Papa! My thoughts cling
to you all, and will not leave their hold. Dearest
Henrietta and Arabel let me be as ever and for
ever

Your fondly attached

Ba

. . . I meant you to have the letters an hour after
I left Wimpole Street. It was very unhappy—I
grieve for it . . . Be happy, my dearest ones—I will
write, be sure.

WIMPOLE STREET WAS THE HOME OF ELIZABETH BARRETT BROWNING

* 35 *

A BROOK IN LINCOLNSHIRE

Not far from Somersby, where Alfred Tennyson was born,
runs the brook that inspired his poem
of the same name.

The Tennyson country, near Somersby, in Lincolnshire, teems with beautiful scenes that the poet used in his verses. The sprawling rectory where he was born is commemorated in "the seven elms, the poplars four, that stand beside my father's door" of the *Ode to Memory*. The spring in the village, called Holy Well, he used dramatically in *Maud*. And finally, near Stockworth Mill, about two or three miles from Somersby, is the famous brook that babbles and chatters through Tennyson's curious poem-and-prose narrative, *The Brook*. The scenery of Lincolnshire is generally quiet and anything but sensational, yet Tennyson has invested its rustic, homely charm with a radiance of its own.

* 3 5 *

Alfred, Lord Tennyson: THE BROOK

I come from haunts of coot and hern,
I make a sudden sally,
And sparkle out among the fern,
To bicker down a valley.

By thirty hills I hurry down,
Or slip between the ridges,
By thirty thorps, a little town,
And half a hundred bridges.

TENNYSON'S BROOK RUNS THROUGH LINCOLNSHIRE FIELDS

36

WELLS CATHEDRAL

The city of Wells, in Somersetshire, was founded by
the Romans. Its beautiful cathedral was built
by bishops between 1171 and 1242.

Over three hundred statues make the west facade of this most lovely of English churches a Bible in stone. Anthony Trollope's *Chronicles of Barsetshire*, a series of six novels, deal with English life in early Victorian times in a small cathedral town like this. The closest approach to Barchester (the seat of Barsetshire) is the town of Wells, with its perfect cathedral and close. St. Cuthbert's church and the Bishop's palace are to the right of the cathedral outside of the picture.

Anthony Trollope: BARCHESTER TOWERS

And so they sauntered forth: first they walked round the old close, according to their avowed intent; then they went under the old arched gateway below St. Cuthbert's little church, and then they turned behind the grounds of the bishop's palace, and so on till they came to the bridge just at the edge of the town. . . .

THE WEST FACADE OF WELLS CATHEDRAL IS ONE OF THE FINEST IN EUROPE

* 37 *

THE MILL AT TEWKESBURY

A mill on the Avon, at Tewkesbury, figures
in two nineteenth-century novels, both
of them written by women.

There is a famous abbey church in the old Gloucestershire town of Tewkesbury, but the literary pilgrim will probably go first to the picturesque mill on the Avon. This first attained fame when Dinah Mulock used it dramatically in *John Halifax, Gentleman*, a moralistic tale that attained wide celebrity. Three years later, when George Eliot published *The Mill on the Floss*, there were those who identified Dorlcote Mill with the one at Tewkesbury. The building is, in its humble way, one of the most picturesque in the western shires, with its high-pitched roof and churning water wheel.

George Eliot: THE MILL ON THE FLOSS

This is Dorlcote Mill. I must stand a minute or
two here on the bridge and look at it, though the
clouds are threatening and it is far on in the after-
noon. The rush of the water, and the booming
of the mill bring a dreamy deafness.

THE MILL AT TEWKESBURY IS PROBABLY THE MILL ON THE FLOSS

✳ 38 ✳

DOONE VALLEY

*The countryside was wilder far when Lorna Doone lived
here with her savage foster relatives in
the seventeenth century.*

Exmoor is a high moorland tract near the Bristol Channel. Its
precipitous hills and small, hidden valleys still have an untamed
quality. Doone Valley, in Devonshire, was in the late seventeenth century nothing more than a robbers' nest, the headquarters of the merciless Doones of Badgeworthy. R. D. Blackmore exaggerated its terrifying aspect in *Lorna Doone*, the story
of a charming girl living unhappily with these desperadoes, her
supposed relatives. But she turns out to be the kidnaped daughter of a Scotch lord and so is free to marry her lover, whose
father had been murdered by the Doones. Blackmore, whose
frank appraisal of his own work is tonic, once dismissed *Lorna
Doone* as "somewhat childish." Possibly it is, but it will never
cease to fascinate children of all ages.

* 38 *

Richard Doddridge Blackmore: LORNA DOONE

. . . a deep green valley, carved from out the mountains in a perfect oval, with a fence of sheer rock standing round it, eighty feet or a hundred high; from whose brink the black wooden hills swept up to the sky-line. A little river glided out from underground with a soft dark babble . . . and fell into the valley. Then, as it ran down the meadow, alders stood on either marge, and grass was blading out upon it, and yellow tufts of rushes gathered.

DOONE VALLEY IS THE SETTING FOR BLACKMORE'S POPULAR NOVEL

* 39 *

STONEHENGE

*This ancient monument on Salisbury Plain
is as mysterious as the cruel forces that
rule the world of Thomas Hardy.*

Emerson was disappointed when he first saw Stonehenge—it looked to him "like a group of brown dwarfs on a wide expanse." But this is a minority report: most people are impressed by its mysterious dignity, which lies, in part, in its hoar antiquity. It is probably four thousand years old. This great circle of huge stones defies explanation: pundits can only guess. The mystery remains. Stonehenge seems the very symbol of the lowering, tragic landscape that is the background of Hardy's powerful Wessex Novels. Folk memory speaks of human sacrifice among these stones, and human sacrifice—to a meaningless destiny— is a theme that obsessed Thomas Hardy.

* 39 *

Thomas Hardy: TESS OF THE D'URBERVILLES

. . . The couple advanced further into this pavil-
ion of the night till they stood in its midst. "It is
Stonehenge!", said Clare. "The heathen temple,
you mean?"
"Yes, older than the centuries; older than the
D'Urbervilles."

STONEHENGE IS A BLEAK STONE RING ON SALISBURY PLAIN

* 40 *

DARTMOOR

Across it, Arthur Conan Doyle's terrible
Hound of the Baskervilles
howled in the night.

Dartmoor, whose rocky hills, treacherous bogs, and heath stretch through Devon, is the setting of Sherlock Holmes' most blood-curdling adventure. Here he solved the mystery of the ghostly hound, an ancient curse of the Baskerville family. One remembers the savage weather Conan Doyle provided for his sleuth as he watched for the hound. A connoisseur in these matters, he was only doing the Dartmoor climate grim justice. An oldtime guidebook describes a storm on the moors as "awful, perilous, astounding, and pitiless, and woe to the stranger who, in a dark night and without a guide, is forced to encounter it!"

* 40 *

Arthur Conan Doyle:
THE HOUND OF THE BASKERVILLES

. . . A low moan had fallen upon our ears . . . On
that side a ridge of rocks ended in a sheer cliff
which over-looked a stone-strewn slope. On its
jagged face was spread-eagled some dark, irregu-
lar object . . . the vague outline hardened into a
definite shape. It was a prostrate man face down-
ward upon the ground, the head doubled under
him at a horrible angle and the body bunched together . . .—the body of Sir Henry Baskerville!

DARTMOOR IS A PLACE OF ROCK AND WASTE LAND

* 41 *

THE THAMES NEAR OXFORD

*Matthew Arnold's Scholar-Gipsy loved to roam
the wooded Cumnor Hills and pensively
stroll along the stripling Thames.*

Arnold was first fascinated by gipsies when he was a boy in the Lake District. In his early twenties, he chanced upon an old legend of "a Lad in the University of Oxford . . . by his poverty forc'd to leave his studies there . . . and joyn himself to a company of Vagabond Gipsies." The Scholar who left the gray towers of Oxford for a roving life in the open countryside never becomes a very convincing gipsy—he has a philosopher's yearning for escape from the noise and distractions of the world. And despite the beautiful descriptions of nature, the whole tone of the poem suggests that Oxford was never very far distant from the Scholar-Gipsy's—and Arnold's—mind. His final love was for Oxford, "home of lost causes . . . and impossible loyalties."

Matthew Arnold: THE SCHOLAR GIPSY

… Men who through those wide fields of breezy grass,
Where black-winged swallows haunt the glittering Thames,
To bathe in the abandoned lasher pass,
Have often passed thee near,
Sitting upon the river bank o'ergrown;

THE THAMES IS A COUNTRY STREAM NEAR OXFORD

* 42 *

READING GAOL

Oscar Wilde served out his sentence of two years'
hard labor and tasted the dregs of misery in
this grim red-brick prison.

In 1895, Oscar Wilde had two successful plays running in
London. At the full tide of glory, he made the great mistake
of his life: against better advice, he sued the Marquess of
Queensberry for criminal libel. The suit failed, and he was
sued in turn on a morals charge. Found guilty, he was sen-
tenced to "two years' hard." In Reading Gaol, in Berkshire,
he wrote *De Profundis*, a moving cry of sustained anguish
which was not published until after his death. He seemed
chastened, and *The Ballad of Reading Gaol*, which he wrote
after his release, suggests purification through suffering. In
Paris, his old spirit returned, somewhat coarsened, though his
deathbed "last words" are—if true—in his best style: "I am
dying beyond my means."

* 42 *

Oscar Wilde: THE BALLAD OF READING GAOL

In Reading gaol by Reading town
There is a pit of shame,
And in it lies a wretched man
Eaten by teeth of flame,
In a burning winding-sheet he lies,
And his grave has got no name.

READING GAOL IS AT READING, IN BERKSHIRE

* 43 *

CLUNBURY VILLAGE

*A. E. Housman wrote with exquisite simplicity of
the people and places of Shropshire,
close to the Welsh border.*

A. E. Housman led a dual life. One segment of his creative energy was devoted to Latin studies, and Cambridge University recognized his greatness as a scholar by making him Kennedy Professor of Latin. Most people, however, know him as the creator of *A Shropshire Lad*, a collection of melodious lyrics of the utmost perfection. Many of these short poems, which sing of the bitterness and implacability of all things beautiful, are about life in the tiny hamlets, incredibly lovely, that lie among the hills of the Severn valley.

* 43 *

A. E. Housman: A SHROPSHIRE LAD

Clunton and Clunbury,
  Clungunford and Clun,
Are the quietest places
  Under the sun.

In valleys of springs of rivers,
  By Ony and Teme and Clun,
The country for easy livers,
  The quietest under the sun,

We still had sorrows to lighten,
  One could not be always glad . . .

CLUNBURY IS AMONG THE LOVELIEST OF ENGLISH HAMLETS

* 44 *

LUDLOW CASTLE

Once a dagger pointed at the heart of Wales,
Ludlow now lies drowsily in the heart of
the peaceful Shropshire Lad country.

Ludlow boasts one of the oldest castles in England, part of it dating from the late eleventh century. As seat of the Lord President of Wales, it teems with historical associations. Literature also claims it for its own. Milton's masque *Comus* was performed in the great hall of the castle in 1634. Samuel Butler, some years later, wrote the first part of his satire *Hudibras* while living in quarters over the gateway. Housman loved Ludlow: in its amphitheater of high ground, it seemed to epitomize the country he never tired of celebrating. He appreciated its homely cheer, too, and when Cambridge "invested in genius" by appointing him professor of Latin, it was observed that "a banquet seems clearly indicated, with much Samian wine and Ludlow beer"—a graceful reference to the two interests that claimed most of his energies. Housman was buried in Ludlow Parish church.

* 44 *

A. E. Housman: A SHROPSHIRE LAD

Leave your home behind, lad,
    And reach your friends your hand,
And go, and luck go with you
    While Ludlow tower shall stand.

· · ·

Come you home a hero,
    Or come not home at all,
The lads you leave will mind you
    Till Ludlow tower shall fall.

And you will list the bugle
    That blows in lands of morn,
And make the foes of England
    Be sorry you were born.

LUDLOW CASTLE IS CLAIMED EQUALLY BY HISTORY AND LETTERS

* 45 *

HADRIAN'S WALL

*It was built by a Roman emperor between the Solway Firth
and the Tyne. It plays a dramatic role in
Kipling's Puck of Pook's Hill.*

Poet of Empire and unexcelled reporter of British life in India,
Rudyard Kipling, great teller of tales, wrote especially memorable children's stories. In *Puck of Pook's Hill*, Puck, usually
a mischievous sprite, appears in the role of a lighthearted
(though earnest) guide to England's mighty past. The children Dan and Una are, through his ability to conjure up the
past, privileged to review that past in a series of dramatic epi-
sodes. One of them is about the great Roman wall that spans
the narrow waist of northern England. Built by Hadrian about
A.D. 120, for centuries it constituted the barrier between bar-
barism and civilization. Hadrian's Wall still marches—seventy-
four miles long—across Northumberland and Cumberland,
often in a state of remarkable preservation.

* 45 *

Rudyard Kipling: PUCK OF POOK'S HILL

"Is it just a Wall? Like the one round the kitchen-garden?" said Dan.

"No, no! It is *the* Wall. Along the top are towers with guard houses, small towers, between. Even on the narrowest part of it three men with shields can walk abreast from guard house to guard house. A little curtain wall, no higher than a man's neck, runs along the top of the thick wall, so that from a distance you see the helmets of the sentries sliding back and forth like beads. Thirty feet high is the Wall, and on the Pict's side, the North, is a ditch, strewn with blades of old swords and spear heads set in wood, and tyres of wheels joined by chains. The Little People come there to steal iron for their arrow-heads."

HADRIAN'S WALL IS FACED WITH SQUARE, HAND-CUT STONES

* 46 *

RUNNYMEDE

*King John's signing of Magna Carta, seven
hundred years ago, was the first great step
towards constitutional government.*

In Surrey, on the north bank of the Thames, lies the level green
meadow of Runnymede. Here John Lackland, the unworthy
son of the great Henry II, in 1215 signed the document that
imposed an epochal check on the tyranny of kings. It was—in
those days when the term "freeman" was rigidly restricted—
the manifesto of an oppressed upper class—the barons. But as
the unwarranted taxes that the King's officers levied on the
barons had ultimately to come from the barons' tenants, Magna
Carta indirectly helped the lower classes. It is the spirit—not
the letter—of Magna Carta that counts, and its spirit has been
invoked in every major fight for constitutional safeguards made
by English-speaking people anywhere. Kipling's poem tells
Englishmen not to forget the meaning of Magna Carta.

Rudyard Kipling: THE REEDS OF RUNNYMEDE

At Runnymede, at Runnymede,
Your rights were won at Runnymede!
No freeman shall be fined or bound,
Or dispossessed of freehold ground,
Except by lawful judgment found
And passed upon him by his peers.
Forget not after all these years,
The Charter signed at Runnymede.

RUNNYMEDE IS A GRASSY PLAIN ON THE BANKS OF THE THAMES

* 47 *

PLYMOUTH HOE

Sir Francis Drake bowled on the Hoe at
Plymouth before sailing against
the Spanish Armada.

"That loftie place at Plimmoth call'd the Hoe" is one of the most beautiful promenades in Great Britain. Today preternaturally spick and span, it was in 1588—Britain's year of crisis —rather more picturesquely shaggy. Here the Lord High Admiral of England—Howard of Effingham—was playing bowls with the other admirals and captains when news came that the Spanish Armada was off the Lizard. Howard wanted to put to sea at once, but Drake interposed: "There's plenty of time to win this game and to thrash the Spaniards too." Drake was right: there was time. No one has captured the boisterous, manly spirit of Devon's great son better than Sir Henry Newbolt in *Drake's Drum*.

Sir Henry John Newbolt: DRAKE'S DRUM

Drake he was a Devon man, an' ruled the Devon Seas,
   (Capten, art tha sleepin' there below?)
Rovin' tho' his death fell, he went wi' heart at ease,
   An' dreamin' arl the time o' Plymouth Hoe.
'Take my drum to England, hang et by the shore,
   Strike et when your powder's runnin' low;
If the Dons sight Devon, I'll quit the port o' Heaven,
   An' drum them up the Channel as we drummed them long ago.'

DRAKE'S STATUE LOOKS TO SEA FROM PLYMOUTH HOE

* 48 *

THE SPANIARDS

An inn, on Hampstead Heath, near London,
was the setting of Alfred Noyes'
poem The Highwayman.

Hampstead Heath, an expanse of wasteland, is enclosed by the suburbs of London. Now highly favored by holiday crowds, it once was a wild tract, the resort of highwaymen and a dangerous spot for the lone traveler. The Spaniards, a tavern on the edge of Hampstead Heath, was the occasional rendezvous of the gentry of the road, as Alfred Noyes' *The Highwayman* recalls. Its curious name may possibly derive from its seventeenth-century landlord, a Spaniard whose unpronounceable name was avoided in the obvious way. The Spaniards lies in the midst of a district alive with historical and literary memories. Dickensians will recall that Mrs. Bardell, Mr. Pickwick's landlady, was arrested here.

Alfred Noyes: THE HIGHWAYMAN

The wind was a torrent of darkness among the gusty trees,
The moon was a ghostly galleon tossed upon cloudy seas,
The road was a ribbon of moonlight over the purple moor,
And the highwayman came riding—
    Riding—Riding—
The highwayman came riding, up to the old inn door.

THE SPANIARDS INN IS ON THE EDGE OF HAMPSTEAD HEATH

✳ 49 ✳

PICCADILLY CIRCUS

It is the hub of the world to Londoners.
English exiles dream of it.

It's a Long, Long Way to Tipperary was the favorite marching song of the first British Expeditionary Force. It became popular in America during the fall and winter of 1914-15. Actually, it was not composed for Tommy Atkins, but—two years before—as a restrained Irish ballad. Its rhythm caught the fancy of the B.E.F., and before long the famous line—"Good-bye, Piccadilly, farewell, Leicester Square"—became elevated by circumstances to the same sentimental pinnacle as Tipperary itself. These localities, which, roughly speaking, are to London what Times Square and Columbus Circle are to New Yorkers, soon became household words in Paris, Baghdad, and Manhattan. Already, some believe *Tipperary* a folk song. But no: it was written by Jack Judge and Harry Williams, otherwise unknown.

* 49 *

POPULAR ENGLISH SONG

It's a long way to Tipperary—it's a long way to go,
It's a long way to Tipperary, to the sweetest girl I know!
Good-bye, Piccadilly, farewell, Leicester Square,
It's a long, long way to Tipperary,
But my heart's right there.

PICCADILLY CIRCUS IS THE HEART OF THE BRITISH EMPIRE

* 50 *

THE THIRTY-NINE STEPS

*A staircase leading to the beach in Kent was the key
to John Buchan's exciting spy story of
World War I.*

John Buchan, afterwards Lord Tweedsmuir and Governor-
General of Canada, was not a great writer, but his books were
honest and gave pleasure to millions of readers. Probably the
most popular of them all, *The Thirty-nine Steps*, concerns the
intrigues of German spies in England just before the outbreak
of World War I. The only clue to the spies' headquarters is a
cryptic sentence scrawled in a dead man's notebook: "Thirty-
nine steps—I counted them—High tide, 10:17 p.m." With this
information, Richard Hannay, the hero, discovers their hide-
out. Buchan had a particular staircase at Broadstairs, on the
Kentish coast, in mind when he wrote the book. It was blown
up by British forces in 1940, to prevent any invading Germans
from reaching the headlands from the beach.

John Buchan: THE THIRTY-NINE STEPS

"Well, gentlemen, I can't think of anywhere else. Of course, there's the Ruff—"

"What's that?" I asked.

"The big chalk headland in Kent, close to Bradgate. It's got a lot of villas on the top, and some of the houses have staircases down to a private beach. It's a very high-toned sort of place, and the residents there like to keep by themselves."

... I closed the book and looked round at the company.

"If one of those staircases has thirty-nine steps we have solved the mystery, gentlemen," I said.

THE THIRTY-NINE STEPS WERE WRECKED DURING ENGLAND'S INVASION SCARE

* ACKNOWLEDGMENT *

The quotation from George Eliot's THE MILL ON THE FLOSS, Picture #37, is reprinted with the permission of Thomas Nelson & Sons.

The quotation from Richard D. Blackmore's LORNA DOONE, Picture #38, is reprinted with the permission of Doubleday, Doran & Co.

The quotation from Thomas Hardy's TESS OF THE D'URBERVILLES, Picture #39, is reprinted with the permission of Harper & Bros.

The quotation from A. Conan Doyle's THE HOUND OF THE BASKER- VILLES, Picture #40, is reprinted with permission of Doubleday, Doran & Co.

The quotation from Matthew Arnold's THE SCHOLAR GYPSY, Picture #41, is reprinted with the permission of The Macmillan Co.

The quotation from Oscar Wilde's THE BALLAD OF READING GAOL, Picture #42, is reprinted with the permission of Thomas Y. Crowell Co.

The quotations from A. E. Housman's A SHROPSHIRE LAD, Pictures #43 and #44, are reprinted by permission of Henry Holt & Co., New York, The Incorporated Society of Authors, Playwrights & Composers, London and Messrs. Jonathan Cape Ltd. of London.

The quotation from Rudyard Kipling's REEDS OF RUNNYMEDE, Pic- ture #46, is from the volume entitled VERSE: INCLUSIVE EDITION, 1885- 1932, Copyright 1891-1934 by Rudyard Kipling, and the quotation from the same author's PUCK OF POOK'S HILL, Picture #45, Copyright 1905-1906 by Rudyard Kipling. Both quotations are reprinted by permission of Doubleday Doran & Co., Inc., New York, The Macmillan Company of Canada, and Mrs. George Bambridge of England.

The quotation from Henry Newbolt's DRAKE'S DRUM, Picture #47, is reprinted by permission of Longman's Green & Co., Inc., New York, Longman's Green & Co., Ltd., London, and Captain Francis Newbolt, Surrey, England.

The quotation from THE HIGHWAYMAN, Picture #48, is from COL- LECTED POEMS by Alfred Noyes, Copyright 1906 by J. B. Lippincott Co., and is reprinted with the publisher's permission, the author's permission, and that of James Blackwood & Co., Ltd., London.

The quotation from IT'S A LONG, LONG WAY TO TIPPERARY, Picture #49, is reprinted with permission of Chappell & Co., Inc., Copyright, 1912, by B. Feldman & Co., London, England.

The quotation from John Buchan's THE THIRTY-NINE STEPS, Picture #50, is reprinted by permission of Houghton Mifflin Co., Boston, the Author's estate, and James Blackwood & Co., Ltd., London.